D1582242

INSPIRED BY NATURE Create beautiful and evocative interiors using the bounty of the natural world. Master stylist and art director Hans Blomquist puts natural materials, items and motifs at the heart of a contemporary decorating style that provides an escape from the noise and haste of modern life and 21st-century technologies. Nature is at the heart of his decorating philosophy, and in the first part of the book Hans shares ideas and inspirations for decorating with flowers, plants, natural objects, materials, textures and colours. Found objects are at the heart of his atmospheric displays, while his rooms are furnished with natural materials such as wood, washed linen, wicker and battered leather. Even his chosen palette – deep indigo, earthy ochre and dusty pink – is based on the subtle hues of the natural world. In the second part of the book, At Home with Nature, Hans visits real-life interiors that possess a sense of comfort, contentment, and beauty and will inspire the reader to create a home that offers a refuge from the wider world as well as the perfect place to welcome family and friends.

SOUTHWARK LIBRARIES

SK 2823261 5

HANS BLOMQUIST

Inspired by
Nature

CREATING A PERSONAL & NATURAL INTERIOR

RYLAND PETERS & SMALL
LONDON • NEW YORK

SENIOR DESIGNER Megan Smith
SENIOR COMMISSIONING EDITOR
Annabel Morgan
EDITOR Zia Mattocks
PRODUCTION Gordana Simakovic
LOCATION RESEARCH Jess Walton

ART DIRECTOR Leslie Harrington
EDITORIAL DIRECTOR Julia Charles
PUBLISHER Cindy Richards

INDEXER Hilary Bird

First published in 2019 by
Ryland Peters & Small
20–21 Jockey's Fields,
London WC1R 4BW
and
Ryland Peters & Small, Inc.
341 E 116th St,
New York, NY 10029
www.rylandpeters.com

10 9 8 7 6 5 4 3

Text © Hans Blomquist 2019
Design and photography
© Ryland Peters & Small 2019

The author's moral rights
have been asserted. All rights
reserved. No part of this
publication may be reproduced,
stored in a retrieval system or
transmitted in any form or by
any means, electronic, mechanical,
photocopying or otherwise,
without the prior permission
of the publisher.

ISBN 978 1 78879 021 5

A catalogue record for this book
is available from the British
Library.

US Library of Congress
cataloging-in-publication data
has been applied for.

Printed and bound in China

contents

Inspired by my love of nature.

The older I get, the more I appreciate the calmness and peace that come from being at one with nature. Where I grew up, in a small village in the south of Sweden, you could walk or cycle everywhere without feeling scared or worrying about getting lost – it was a very free, unconfined way to grow up. The garden of my childhood home backs onto a forest and I spent most of my time there, playing and running around with my friends. To us, it was like the largest playground ever, a true luxury. Unlike my friends, I was always looking for interesting things, collecting branches and stones, picking flowers, looking at birds and sometimes digging up a small tree I liked and replanting it next to our garden. Living so close to nature definitely sparked my love for the natural world, and this was reinforced by our frequent visits to my grandmother. It was heavenly to be in her garden with all its flowers, vegetables and berries that she tended with so much care. I loved sitting with her

in her hammock, looking at everything growing around us and listening to her stories. She loved cycling around the picturesque countryside where she lived, picking mushrooms and wild berries, and I first saw the beauty of nature through her eyes, which undoubtedly influences how I still see things. In the summer, we swam or fished from my grandfather's rowing boat on a nearby lake, which was as quiet and still as a mirror. I had an amazing childhood, surrounded by people who valued and cherished nature, and the love I feel for nature today most certainly stems from everything they showed me and from all the adventures I was lucky enough to experience. I am so grateful to have grown up immersed in nature – a mystical, ever-changing world where you can get lost for hours and hours just being yourself and feeling at one with the trees, the sun, the wind, the smells and the beauty of the natural world.

Nature
all year round.

spring

It is a very special feeling when the light starts to return after a long, dark winter. The daylight extends by minutes every day without me really noticing, but then, all of a sudden, it is so obvious both to my eyes and my senses. For me, this is most impactful in Sweden, where the winter is so long and feels as though it will never end. Every year I am grateful to have got through yet another winter to meet the spring light and everything that comes with it, such as the first flowers covering the ground in the still-naked forest. It fills me with such happiness and calmness, and makes me feel reborn.

BRING SPRING INSIDE.
Every spring, when flowers start to grow in the forest and along the country roads, and when the first batch of blooms appears in the florist's, I immediately fill my home with either a large bouquet of peonies (opposite) or some simple but beautiful wild garlic/ramp flowers from my garden (this page).

the softness of spring

The colours and shapes of spring flowers are so delicate and soft, ranging from the whitest white to the palest pink and the deepest blue, and set off by the vibrant colour and texture of their green leaves. I would not be able to choose a favourite out of all the glorious spring flowers that delight us each year, but there are some that have a special place in my heart, as they have surrounded me since my childhood and are for me synonymous with the early days of spring. I have very fond and vivid memories of my mother going out every year to pick wood anemones and putting the delicate flowers in a very small glass or an eggcup on the dining table to celebrate spring. To this day, I still love driving around the winding country lanes when the lupins are in full bloom, in an explosion of the most beautiful colours – shades of white, purple, blue and pink.

A LIFE OF THEIR OWN.
When the first tulips arrive in the florist's soon after Christmas, it is hard to resist buying a bunch to celebrate that spring is just around the corner. The amazing colours and shapes they take on become more beguiling the longer you keep them.

ON DISPLAY.

Even the simplest arrangement of spring flowers in glass vases will be eye-catching and add texture, colour and a touch of spring to your home. You can place them anywhere, on their own or as part of a display. Clockwise from left are bluebells, bringing vitality to a very simple tableau; poppies still waiting to open; and a small chestnut branch adding colour and shape to a rustic still life. Overleaf are peonies in the softer, dustier shades of pink, which have a vintage feel and sit well in a darker, moody setting, such as on this stack of old grain sacks on an antique chair.

delicate white

Some of the best things in life are free – especially everything that comes from nature. There is a such a treasure chest out there in every season, but particularly in spring when the natural world around us simply erupts into leafy greens and delicate blossoms, and it is all there for us to enjoy on a country walk or when driving through the countryside. I have a hard time resisting the urge to pick something up and bring it home, as I believe there is nothing as beautiful as what nature creates of its own accord, without being forced-grown or overproduced. The way in which flowers, plants and trees grow naturally is hard to replicate, and it is impossible to get them to grow as poetically as they do when left to their own devices. Many varieties of intricate white blossoms appear in spring, offset by the lushest spring green, and this purest of colour combinations will add freshness to any kind of setting in your home.

CENTRE STAGE.
Cow parsley has to be one of my best-loved wild flowers because
it grows everywhere in early spring, swaying in the wind on tall, wiry
stems. I often bring home a large bunch and place it in a simple glass
vase without arranging it, to recreate the same look as when it grows
beside the road (opposite, left). White chestnut flowers (opposite, right)
and fruit-blossom branches (above left) make a grand statement in the
home as a large display on a side table, while a bouquet of early sweet
peas (above right) gives life to any area. Overleaf are wood anemones (left),
my childhood favourite, and a blossoming branch, perfectly at home
in a pure white jug (right).

summer

I am torn when it comes to summer.
Part of me loves the lush greenery,
summer flowers, large rosebushes and
overgrown wild gardens where you are
surrounded by tall, leafy trees, bushes,
flowers and grass. Another part of me
loves the desert with its vast landscape
where you can see for miles, and where
everything is dry and dusty, and
punctuated by cactuses, sparse trees,
scrubby bushes and tumbleweed.
There is also something about the
light and the smells in the desert that
is so appealing to me, and I guess my
soft spot for it is because of its stark
contrast to the verdant summers
in Sweden where I grew up.

DESERT DRAMA.
I am lucky enough to have a house in the south
of France, where most summers are hot and dry.
On my walks along the country lanes around my
house, I always find dried flowers and bushes that
remind me of the desert. Once brought home and
set against the greyish walls and neutral linen
textiles, they create an evocative desert vibe.

summer display

Creating a display can seem daunting if you don't know where to start, so first decide what kind of effect you would like and what feeling you want it to evoke. Trust me, it need not be complicated. A display in your home can range from a simple and modest floral arrangement to something more eye-catching and oversized, or it can incorporate some of your favourite objects gathered on a small table, stool or bench. For a successful summer display, start by choosing nature as the centrepiece and then add other elements that will support your focal point in terms of colour, texture and shape. In your own home, anything is allowed and it is only you who can decide whether it looks right or wrong.

SUN-BLESSED SCENES.

Fennel grows wild in my garden in the south of France and every summer I bring in a large, tall bunch, as I love both its colour and aroma (opposite, left). A simple still life of sun-bleached wood, dried hydrangeas and vintage shoe moulds creates a summery feeling (opposite, right). Dried summer grasses have been tied to a wooden stick suspended on linen string to make a textural wall decoration (below left). Overblown and nearly dried echinacea flowers in a simple glass tumbler add a summertime look to a side-table display (below right).

TRAVEL TROPHIES.
I bring a lot of things home from my travels, most of which I have found along the road, on a walk or by the beach, such as these beautiful cactus skeletons, which sit perfectly in a tonal display with dried sea sponges and a vintage straw hat (this page). A wooden stool is used to display feathers gathered in hand-carved wooden vessels from Africa (opposite).

CUT AND DRIED.

Every second or third year, sunflowers are planted in the fields around our house in the south of France. It is one of the most beautiful sights, as they all stand so tall, facing the morning sun. There are always a few growing wild, too, and I am quick to pick them to add some of that bright sunshine yellow to my home. I don't throw them away when they have dried out, since they look just as beautiful then as when they are in full bloom (this page). Displayed on a marble mantelpiece is a vintage glass vase filled with dried poppies found on one of our daily walks through the fields with our whippet, Felix (opposite). The hand-painted wooden goose was bought in a flea market on a work trip to Tucson, Arizona.

autumn

As the days start to grow shorter, I feel a little sad that the long summer days are coming to an end, but there is so much beauty to follow that after a few weeks I am loving all the colours that the new season brings and the rich scent of the forest after the rain. I have learned to love autumn for the colours, the quiet walks in the forest gathering mushrooms and the beautiful light through the trees when the sun is low in the sky.

LESS IS MORE.
You don't need armfuls of flowers or foliage to create an impact in your home. Sometimes just a handful of stems allows you to appreciate the intricate beauty of nature.

autumnal display

If you like the autumnal colour palette of dried leaves, dried flowers and other natural found objects, it is easy to create a long-lasting still life in any part of your home. It can be a large arrangement on a sideboard or a small one on your coffee table, where you will see it every day as you curl up on the sofa to read or snooze. Creating a display with found objects from nature mixed with other items will make a scene that is easy to change or update with new items when you find them or another large branch with dried leaves. Using backdrops in the same colour scheme will make your display look like an oil painting and is also very Instagram-friendly.

CURATED COMPOSITIONS.
Dried branches, flowers and gourds are the natural elements that will give your still life a very personal touch, as well as introducing an extra layer of texture, shape and colour. I can guarantee that only you will have this exact composition, because there are no branches or flowers that will look exactly like the ones you have gathered. Incorporating wooden objects into your still life will give you different shapes, textures and shades of the autumnal colour scheme to play with, while tall branches will create height, resulting in a more interesting display.

TEXTURAL CONTAINERS.
When it comes to displaying dried branches,
grasses and flowers, you don't have to use a vase
or other container that holds water, as they won't
need any. So you can go all out and be as creative
as you like. I love using woven baskets to hold
dried branches, which themselves add another
layer of texture to the home.

winter

When the sun is shining in a clear blue sky, and the ground and trees are covered in glistening snow, winter is stunningly beautiful. But these days seem to be few and far between, and winter mostly tends to be damp, rainy and grey. I am lucky that I get to travel to warmer places during the winter for work, so I really appreciate the few winter days I spend at home, curled up in an armchair by the fire with lit candles all around.

ARCHITECTURAL BRANCHES.
During the winter season I mostly like to decorate with dried branches. Small branches with dried flowers or seedpods as well as larger birch branches create a display that will last you well through the winter.

wintry evergreens

For natural displays during the winter season, I tend to use dried branches and pieces of greenery that have a slightly greyish tone, which echoes both the wintry light and the nature surrounding us during these darker months. There are still a lot of natural treasures to be found and brought home during this time of year, as there are all the pine trees with their spiky leaves and pine cones, which can look enchanting, especially the bigger branches, and mostly last throughout the entire winter. I love the effect of a beautiful pine branch, for example, or wiry birch branches in a simple vase. The winter season also has a lot of flowers to offer, but I prefer to try and wait for the spring to arrive before I bring any home. For the most part, I think one should enjoy the things that are in season, to stay in tune with the natural cycle, and refrain from using flowers and plants that have been forced to grow just for us, when they would not start to grow naturally outside until months later.

NEEDLES AND CONES.
A pine branch bearing pine cones sits well in a simple glass vase and will look as handsome dried as when it was first brought in. Use it as part of an everyday still life to add a long-lasting natural element to your home during the winter months.

LASTING PLEASURES.
Larch and eucalyptus are the perfect greyish green that I love to use in winter. You can hang branches on a wall to dry (above left) or put them in a vase. I mixed dried birch branches with the eucalyptus to give this bouquet more life (left); they will both dry beautifully and last a long time. A simple succulent of the same colour will look stunning all year round (above). Overleaf, a dried larch branch with pine cones makes a natural wall decoration (left), while a simple vase holds delicate seedheads as part of a wintry scheme (right).

SEASONAL SCENTS

Scent is such a personal thing and I find every home has its own special smell without adding anything. But sometimes it is nice to introduce another scent into your home, either to set a special mood or just to reflect the current season with a particular fragrance. I mostly use natural flowers and foliage to fill my home with real, pure scent, which I prefer to the sometimes heavy aromas of scented candles or incense. In addition to perfumed plants, flowers and candles, a home is also scented by the food you cook. Toasted bread is one of my favourite smells when I visit someone's house, while newly washed wooden floors is one of those scents that I truly love to come home to.

ATMOSPHERIC AROMA.
Eucalyptus is a scent I adore in my home, and when you have a vase
of eucalyptus branches in the bathroom while you shower, the room
becomes filled with their beautiful perfume (opposite, left). Sage
is an easy herb to grow and dry, and burning a small sprig will quickly
scent the entire home (opposite, right). When it comes to scented candles,
fig tree is my number-one choice; it is a fragrance I never tire of (below
left). In spring, paperwhites are my favourite scented flower and just
a few blooms can make a whole room smell truly amazing (below right).

Decorating
with nature.

Nature's *colours*

You simply can't go wrong when decorating with a colour inspired by nature. It will create an interior that is so calm and easy to live in because nature's colours all work in harmony with each other. You can choose a muted, darker, moodier, lighter or brighter scheme, and everything will all sit well together, whether you decide to keep things tonal or use contrasting colours.

natural tones

Nature is the greatest source of colour inspiration for any interior you want to decorate. Whether you are designing a colour scheme for a whole room or just adding in some textiles or creating a still life, if you take your inspiration from tones found in nature, you will achieve great results and create an interior you can live with for a very long time. I tend to prefer more muted natural tones, as they give a room a very soothing and peaceful look in any kind of light. The softer, gentler colours of spring florals and brighter summer accents are, in my opinion, best brought into your home in the shape of textiles and decorative objects, as they will work well to add colour to a neutral and natural colour scheme. The more sober, pared-back shades of autumn and winter are perfect for wall colours and also for textiles, furniture and decorative pieces.

FOUND IN NATURE.
I can happily spend hours on a country road, in a field or a forest, searching for interesting and beautiful objects to use for colour inspirations or as decorative items, such as this wasps' nest (this page) or the large dried plant hanging on my bedroom wall in the south of France (opposite).

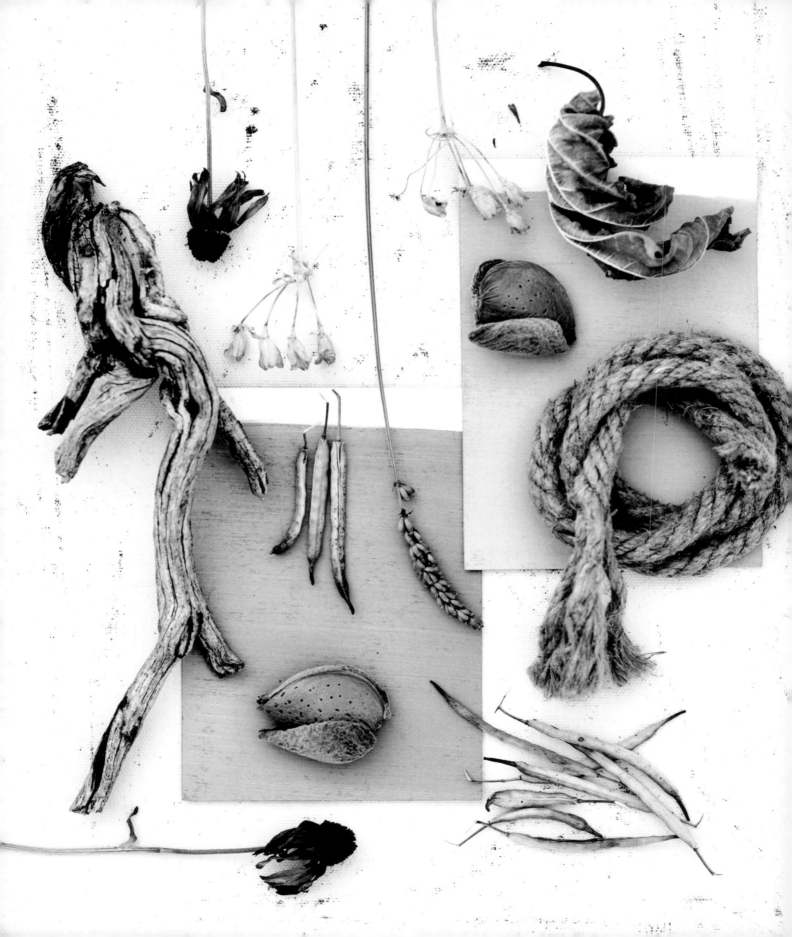

INSPIRED BY NATURE.
You can find every single colour in nature that you might want
to include on a mood board or inspiration board for an interior
colour scheme. There are a million variations of flowers, grasses,
leaves and wood in as many different textures and colours, and
drawing on them for design ideas will ensure a perfect result.
Here, a large still life was inspired by the tones of the natural
world (opposite), where all the objects and hues work in harmony
and are subtle and soothing to look at and live with. The wall is
painted in Chaff by Bauwerk Colour (this page).

dusty pastels

The soft tones of dusty pastels, inspired by flowers such as fading peonies, dried hydrangeas and spring blossoms, are a great source of ideas when choosing accent colours for the home. They have a softer look compared to pure pastels, so I always look for pastel shades that contain a dash of black pigment. In fact, I naturally gravitate towards paints from the 'dirtier' or muddier side of a colour chart rather than the purer tones, as they are easier to live with and decorate around. Dusty pastel colours are widely available in the shape of textiles but also work well as wall colours, making an easy backdrop for wooden furniture or neutral upholstery.

PRETTY PASTELS.
Softly coloured linen napkins and bed linen will give your dining table and bedroom an uplifting, spring-like feeling (above). This pastel pink painted wall has kept its colour for more than a hundred years and still looks beautiful (opposite). Textiles inspired by the true colours of nature work equally well in a neutral colour scheme as with darker and moodier colours; play with floral patterns and large blossom branches to give your bedroom or living room a pretty springtime look (overleaf).

dark & moody

When decorating a room from scratch, it can be quite hard to decide what colour to go for on the walls and floors. Whiter and lighter shades tend to be my first choice for a main colour, with darker tones and textures brought in to add life to the room and prevent it from looking bland. My apartment in Paris is all white with a very old herringbone wood floor. The furniture is also mostly light and neutral with textures of wood and some metal, and I really like it that way. However, I decided to experiment with a moodier colour scheme in my house in the south of France, so I repainted the walls in a dusty greyish colour and I love the effect – it feels calm and intimate and somehow the light is even more beautiful. So don't be afraid to go for a darker, more sober look as it feels so good to live in.

LIGHT AND SHADE.
Interior designer Marie Olsson Nylander has used a dark wall colour as the basis of her decorative scheme and brightened it up with lighter accents (opposite). She also used a large mirror to bounce light around the space (above left). Pale textiles will brighten up a room in an effortless way (above right). Light-coloured flowers and a neutral dried plant can illuminate dark walls and make them easier to live with (overleaf).

burnt & earthy

Colours inspired by spices have a burnt and earthy feel. Cumin, paprika and saffron are a few of those shades, and can be used in interiors both as the main colour and as accents, to create a look that is rich and earthy but at the same time very colourful. These natural tones have a slightly higher density of black pigment, which makes them not too bright and invasive to use as a main colour in your home. However, I tend to believe that these colours work better in a hotter climate than in a cooler one, as the warm hues glow invitingly on bright, clear days and give a soothing effect when warm sunlight is streaming in through the windows.

SPICING IT UP.
Neutral and white decorative objects sit easily against the coloured wall, painted in Kelp from Bauwerk Colour, inspired by saffron (above left). Spices and dried autumn leaves are perfect components for a mood board illustrating a burnt and earthy look (above right and opposite). The wall overleaf has been painted in Bauwerk Colour's lime paint in Pheasant, which is ideal for applying in this textural way to add character to an interior.

Textures & *materials*

To create a truly natural look, I believe you have to use both different textures and materials. To achieve the right effect, mix wood with metal, glass with soft and shaggy textiles, and plain coloured walls with worn and used wood. The contrast and the patina add life, interest and depth, and make your home feel truly natural. The various elements will support each other as long as they are all made of materials sourced from nature.

wood

If I had to choose one material, I think it would have to be wood – even though I love stone, metal and textiles just as much. Wood is a material that lasts forever, and the more you use it and let it age over time, the more beautiful it will become. Every dining table I have ever owned has been made of antique wood, and I love the traces of past times you can see on the surface – stains from dinners enjoyed, glass rings soaked into the surface, and bumps and scratches that have been softened by the passage of time. Wood is one of the only materials that ages this well – unlike many materials, it just looks better and better the more it is used.

WOOD AS A BACKDROP.
This bedroom features a wall covered from floor to ceiling in birch plywood (opposite). Impactful without being intrusive or taking over the space, it gives a warm and natural backdrop that will age well with time. The shelving unit (above right) covers an entire wall, which looks striking and provides plenty of room to display treasured belongings. The leather stool (above left) functions as a bedside table and adds another layer of texture to the wooden wall, sisal rug and soft vintage linen.

ELEMENTAL LIVING.
A very simple armchair that offers low seating is the main feature of this pared-down living room (opposite). Layers of texture have been added with a soft white linen throw and a more robust piece of woven linen fabric as a rug. The raw wooden stool (this page) introduces another element of texture and material to the space, along with the large dried palm leaf leaning against the wall. This is painted in Drift lime paint from Bauwerk Colour, one of nine colours that I created for them.

PAINTED OR RAW.

I think wood works as well painted as raw in an interior, so don't be afraid to use painted wooden furniture or let it age naturally with time. An antique chest of drawers with peeling paint should never be restored; just leave it as it is and its unique texture will bring life and visual interest to even the most pristine backdrop (above). A raw wooden bench can be used as a display surface in any room, while a vintage metal basket is the perfect container for storing firewood, as the beautiful colour and texture of the kindling and logs can still be seen and appreciated (opposite).

EVERYDAY WOOD.
This wooden planked wall (opposite) has such a handsome, timeworn patina, created through years of exposure to the elements. Layered with more wood, ceramics and textiles, this setting is as close as it comes to natural perfection – even though nothing about this scene is 'perfect'. A collection of wooden utensils, boards and trays will add rustic texture to any dining table (above right and left). These small bark vessels were made by a friend, inspired by the old-fashioned cups used to drink water when working outside in a field or by a river (left).

THE PATINA OF AGE

At the risk of repeating myself, when it comes to everyday living and how we use both practical items and decorative objects in our homes, I can only reiterate that when something bears the traces of time it is just too beautiful to throw away. Every day, I cherish the pieces I own because of their history and the stories they tell. But modern society encourages us to throw away things once they grow old, or stained, chipped or scraped, and this is not something we can keep on doing. We have to think a step ahead and start to love and value the things we have – for the sake of ourselves, the environment and our planet. 'Recycle, reuse, reduce' should be everyone's motto.

TREASURED WOOD.

I found this large wooden chopping board at a flea market in the south of France (opposite, left). I use it every day when I am there and would never replace it with a new one. The herringbone-pattern parquet floor of my apartment in Paris was laid in 1850 when the house was built (opposite, right). It is very uneven and quite noisy to walk on but utterly beautiful. I don't know what made the circular stain on my dining table in Paris and it doesn't really matter, I just find it charming to look at each day (below left). This raw, untreated piece of wood with cracks and stains has been attached to a metal structure to make a perfect side table (below right).

china & porcelain

My china of choice is nearly always pure white and I have a special love for vintage restaurant china, as the quality is amazing – the pieces are heavy and will last a lifetime. I don't go to as many flea markets today as I did a few years ago, given that I already have more than I need, but when I do go I have a very hard time resisting buying yet more white ceramic plates, bowls, platters and jugs! At some point you have to exert some self-control and accept that you have enough, but still, once in a while, I find something I believe I can't live without (although deep down I know I really could) and I add another piece or two to my already large collection. One of my greatest pleasures is to set my dining table with pure white china on a soft, rumpled linen tablecloth – the result is truly beautiful.

A DAILY STILL LIFE.

You can make a still life out of almost anything you have at home. Cake stands together with simple ceramic cups, some delicate small plates and sculptural spoons make a simple yet practical still life (opposite). I bought the bowls (above left) on a work trip to China and they instantly evoke memories of that excursion. I love the heavy white plates and Chinese-inspired spoons made out of clay (above right), which were photographed in a house in Marrakech (see pages 118–133). Eggs always taste best when they are eaten with a porcelain spoon (left); the oval plate is part of my vintage collection of original restaurant tableware.

metal work

I love the craftsmanship of metalwork and am always in awe of how metalsmiths can fashion any shape or form to create pieces that are both useful and decorative. I think I could legitimately call myself a collector of anything made out of metal, and in particular zinc. I guess it is the patina of vintage metal pieces that speaks to me and catches my eye whenever I am roaming around a flea market or antiques fair. Zinc is one of those materials, like wood, that I appreciate even more when I can see how much the item has been used and cherished. Well-made metal pieces, whatever they are, tend to last a lifetime, even when they are subjected to heavy everyday use or left out in the garden to weather the elements.

METALLIC CHARMS.

The metal chair is one of many I have collected over the years in France (opposite, left); no longer used as a chair, it has now become a decorative feature, holding a French flag. The beautiful metal and glass lantern from India is in constant use in our apartment in Paris (opposite, right). A metal topiary that I bought years ago when living in London is still one of my favourite possessions, and the zinc box is useful for storage but also makes an attractive planter (below left). I love the suspended metal rail holding these copper saucepans (below right) – a practical solution for storing pots and pans if you have limited cupboard space and it keeps the work surface free from clutter.

glass

It is easy to forget how much glass surrounds us every day, most importantly in the windows of our homes, which protect us from the outside but still allow us to see out and let the natural light shine through. I love decorating with glass because of the way it catches the light, and you can use different shapes and forms to create the most exquisite still lifes. I have many childhood memories of visiting glassworks near where we lived in Sweden and watching the glass-blowers make anything from everyday drinking glasses to amazing sculptural pieces. I have enormous respect for the craft and I hope most people would choose hand-blown over mass-produced glassware.

ALL CLEAR.
Vintage glassware is still easy to find at flea markets and I can always find room for more pieces. A collection of vintage storage jars and a flask holding dried branches make a simple still life (above left). I love how prettily newly washed glassware reflects the light (above right). When we stayed with our friends at Bauwerk Colour, I lay in bed in the morning admiring this collection of vintage glass bottles on the windowsill (opposite); the brown bottles look jewel-like when the light hits them.

woven textures

I am amazed by how many items and objects can be fashioned out of materials such as straw, grass, bamboo and rattan. It seems as if there are no limits to what can be made. You will find everything from furniture to baskets, storage chests, lampshades and lamp stands – you name it and it can most likely be created with the traditional skills and craftsmanship that have been used for hundreds of years and are still evolving. The textures and sculptural shapes that woven items bring to an interior have a different quality and character from other materials. They can be heavily woven and sturdy or made with finesse for a light and airy effect. Any items woven from natural fibres that you introduce into your home will add texture and interesting shapes to complement any style of interior, whether it is a very minimal space or a highly decorated one. Woven textures are also sturdy and, if used in the correct way and with the right care, they will last a lifetime.

VARIETY AND VERSATILITY.
I have a real soft spot for woven baskets, as I like the easy way they add texture and form to a space, and today you can find them made from so many different types of natural fibres and in endless shapes. Fine and lightweight baskets can be used as simple decorative pieces, bowls or lampshades, while heavyweight baskets are practical all around the home for storing magazines, cushions, blankets and fabrics or rolls of papers and posters. They are versatile, easy to move and always come in handy.

Natural
textiles

One of the elements in your home that you can't be without, textiles make a home personal, soft and cosy. They add colour and texture, and are easy to update whenever you feel the need for a new look or just want to change the vibe of your home to reflect the new season. There is a huge variety of different compositions and weights, textures and finishes, and colours and patterns to choose from when looking for textiles for your home, but I prefer to use only natural materials such as linen, cotton and wool.

soft linen

I mostly go for linen when choosing fabric for my own home. I love how this natural material feels and how easy it is to style to create a relaxed look. I am very lazy when it comes to ironing – even my clothes – and linen is one of the only materials that can be left wrinkled and still look soft and natural, rather than messy or unstyled. There is a lot to choose from when it comes to linen: heavy weaves, lighter weaves, dyed or natural. I love them all and you can never have too much linen as it is such a versatile fabric. I use it as tablecloths, cushions, curtains and loose covers or upholstery for my armchairs and footstools. Linen is so easy to live with, as it washes well and looks better and feels softer every time, with the large bonus of never having to be ironed or fussed over.

LAID-BACK LOOKS.
I use linen fabric everywhere at home. In our house in the south of France (above), we opted for a very effortless, relaxed look, with bleached linen cushions mixed with neutral unbleached linen covers on the sofas and armchairs. At home in Paris, this pink linen tablecloth is the perfect colour to use in springtime, when I like to accessorize it with branches of cherry blossom (opposite).

CELEBRATE EVERY DAY.
Every day should feel special and every meal should be treated like a celebration, even if you are just eating a bowl of pasta or a boiled egg. Easy-to-wash linen makes it easy to create an inviting and festive everyday table setting. When we lay our table at home for breakfast, lunch or dinner, we always use a tablecloth to make the meal feel more special (this page). A large linen tablecloth is very simple to make from linen fabric or can be bought ready-made, while inexpensive linen napkins are easy to find. A simple still life of some of my linen fabrics and cushion covers waiting to be used or placed around the house (opposite).

COSY & COMFY

The quickest way to make a home look cosier and more welcoming is to introduce a variety of different textiles – fabrics, rugs and sheepskins, either layered or used on their own. Whether you mix heavy woven wool with sheepskin or a shaggy rug with soft linen, everything works and whatever combinations you decide on will make your home a softer, warmer place to live in. By mixing materials and different kinds of weaves, you can create a look that is more layered and textured. Using textiles all in the same colour might sound uninspiring, but if you choose to layer up a mix of materials, weaves and weights, the effect will be anything but boring.

SOFT SPOTS.

Mixing different textures and styles of textiles on sofas, armchairs, dining chairs, floors or tables will add interest to a room. For instance, layer a heavy woven wool cushion with a fur pillow on a simple, light, vintage linen sofa cover (opposite, left). Rugs will help to keep your home warm and cosy in winter, especially if your floors are not well insulated (opposite, right). Layer different fabrics along with sheepskin or goatskin on the end of your bed for even more tactile layers (below left). In winter, we add sheepskins to our dining chairs in Paris, which bring another element of texture to the white room and provide extra warmth and comfort (below right).

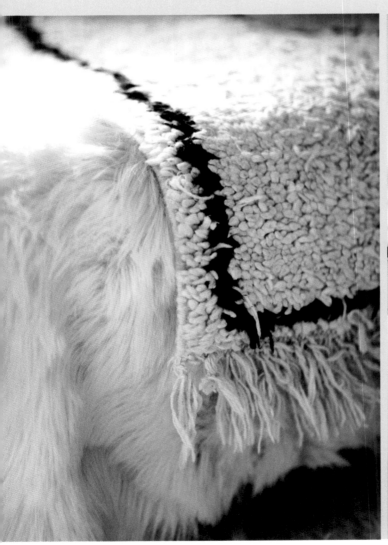

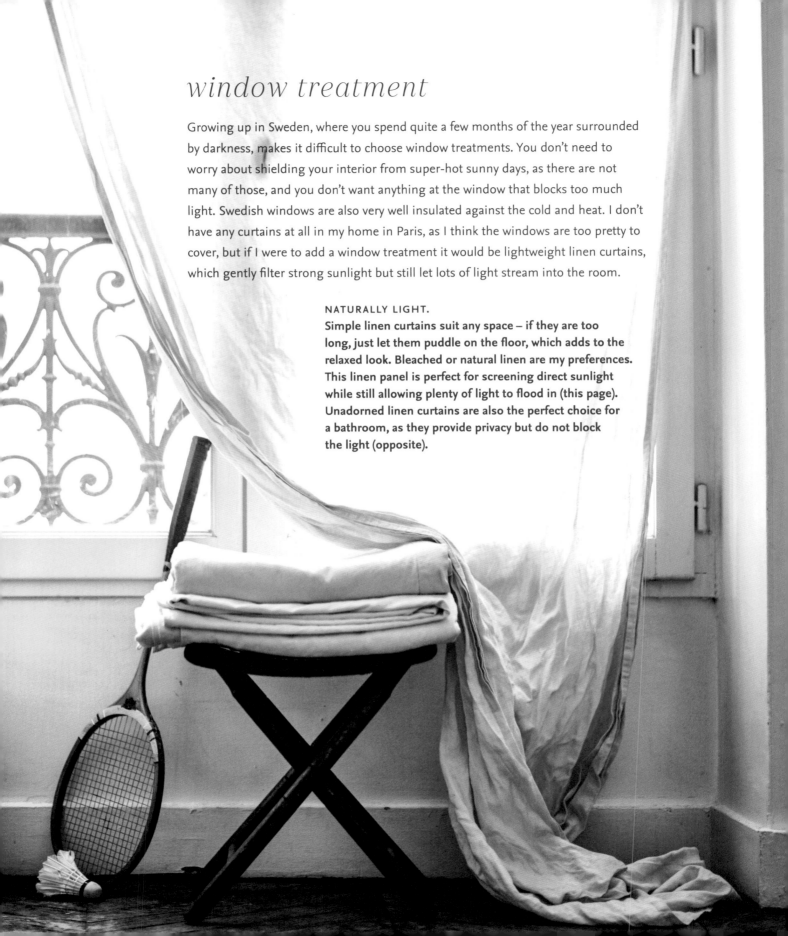

window treatment

Growing up in Sweden, where you spend quite a few months of the year surrounded by darkness, makes it difficult to choose window treatments. You don't need to worry about shielding your interior from super-hot sunny days, as there are not many of those, and you don't want anything at the window that blocks too much light. Swedish windows are also very well insulated against the cold and heat. I don't have any curtains at all in my home in Paris, as I think the windows are too pretty to cover, but if I were to add a window treatment it would be lightweight linen curtains, which gently filter strong sunlight but still let lots of light stream into the room.

NATURALLY LIGHT.
Simple linen curtains suit any space – if they are too long, just let them puddle on the floor, which adds to the relaxed look. Bleached or natural linen are my preferences. This linen panel is perfect for screening direct sunlight while still allowing plenty of light to flood in (this page). Unadorned linen curtains are also the perfect choice for a bathroom, as they provide privacy but do not block the light (opposite).

TONAL SETTING.
Showing off some of my linen
tablecloths on a vintage ladder
makes a beautiful still life and
means they are always within easy
reach (this page). We set the table
in our house in the south of
France like this pretty much every
day (opposite): a bleached vintage
linen tablecloth with linen napkins
and vintage white china. The metal
candlesticks add contrast to the
predominantly white-dressed table
and we light them for every meal
– breakfast, lunch and dinner –
all year round.

indigo blues

Aside from neutral and bleached linen, indigo blues are my preferred colours for linen. In fact, whenever I am asked what my favourite colour is, without hesitation my answer is always blue. Indigo mixes well with most other colours that I use in my own homes – the natural shades and the soft whites and greys in particular. It adds a layer of interest and depth to interiors that are fairly light and where a lot of neutral tones are used. I have been thinking of learning to dye my own indigo fabric so that I can start experimenting with different dyes and create my own patterns, but I have not got around to it yet. I guess it is one of those things that I tell myself I can put off until I have some time off or I retire. But when I go on holiday I am far too lazy and like to spend my time sitting under a tree, luxuriating in the silence. Somehow, knowing I could be doing so much makes me do close to nothing. One day, though, I am determined to learn to dye perfect indigo fabric, but in the meantime, there are so many beautiful examples out there for me to add to my collection.

STUDIES IN BLUE.

If I don't set my dining table in all white, I go for indigo blue linens and use mostly wood instead of white china. The combination is so pleasing and gives a rustic and very elegant Japanesque look (opposite, left).

A stack of some of my favourite blue cushion covers that moved in with me after one of my photoshoots (opposite, right). Our dining table in the south of France was one of the first things we bought when we moved in. It is a long, wooden farmhouse table painted in a beautiful blue-grey colour that makes it easy to set the table with any kind of table linen or tableware (above left). This still life comprises a small wooden chair with an indigo throw and a simple wooden stool standing on a heavyweight linen cloth, painted in a dark indigo blue and turned upside down to expose the uneven paint that has soaked through (above right).

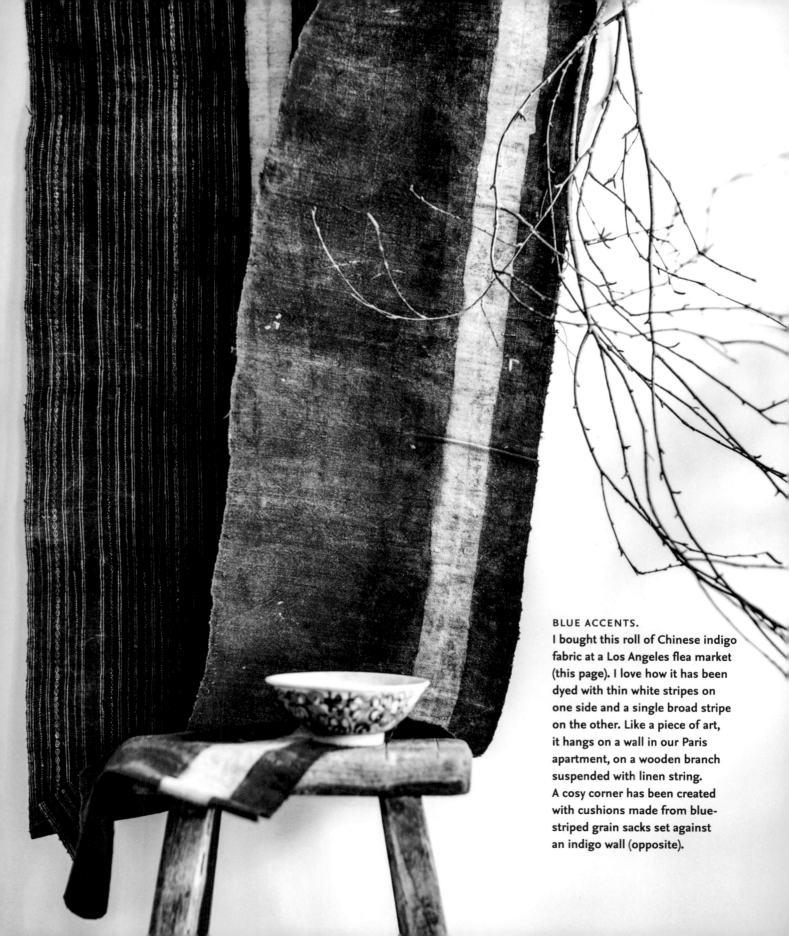

BLUE ACCENTS.
I bought this roll of Chinese indigo fabric at a Los Angeles flea market (this page). I love how it has been dyed with thin white stripes on one side and a single broad stripe on the other. Like a piece of art, it hangs on a wall in our Paris apartment, on a wooden branch suspended with linen string. A cosy corner has been created with cushions made from blue-striped grain sacks set against an indigo wall (opposite).

colour & pattern

I am very drawn to handwoven rugs and throws in deep, burnt colours, which I have grown to love the more I have used them in my work as an interior stylist. The look reminds me of the traditional style of Native Americans and cowboys, but at the same time it feels new and exciting to use, with its patterns and colours bringing depth and personality to any interior space, whether modern or rustic. I am a true believer that nobody has only one interior style that they like, and yet it is easy to be influenced by trends without thinking about what you really want. But trends change rapidly, so your home should primarily reflect your personality and contain the things you love, whether they are in fashion or not.

WOVEN WONDERS.
In a Los Angeles home full of amazing collections (see pages 162–175), colourfully patterned woven rugs are piled on top of a cowhide cushion on a vintage distressed wooden trunk (above left). Handwoven rugs come in so many sizes, patterns and colours that the choice can seem overwhelming. This one is beautifully accessorized by a vintage wooden bowl and some sculptural horns (above right). A handwoven throw completes the inviting mix of colours and patterns on this suspended sofa (opposite).

Decorative
still lifes

A still life is simply a collection of a few favourite objects arranged together in a pleasing way on any kind of surface, such as a sideboard, mantelpiece, coffee table or small side table. But it could also be part of a larger setting with furniture, an everyday vignette that is still just as much of a still life as a group of smaller items. We create such still lifes all around the home without consciously thinking about it. A routine table setting or even the items that collect on a kitchen work surface, for example, could be considered still lifes.

natural gatherings

Walking along a beach, in a forest, through fields or even in a city park, you will always find something that nature has created that you can incorporate in an existing still life or use as the inspiration for a new one. There is so much beauty in nature and every single thing you find will be very different from the last one you picked up – on a beach, for instance, each seashell and pebble will vary in colour, size and shape. There is always something worth bringing home to use in a picture or add to a still life, so I always keep my eyes open and collect everything from bleached driftwood, a shell or a pebble on the beach, to a branch or dried plant on forest walks.

GIFTS FROM NATURE.
Dead plants and abandoned nests look so sculptural alongside other natural treasures (previous pages). Mussel shells, dried seaweed and smooth, bleached branches make a simple but effective still life on any free surface (opposite). Sunflowers are one of my favourite flowers and still look beautiful when they are totally dried out (above left). Smooth, dark grey pebbles decorated with thin pieces of bamboo are displayed in a small wooden bowl on a coffee table (above right).

ON A LARGER SCALE.

If you step back in your home and look at the bigger picture, you will see that there are large-scale still lifes all around us. Everything on this kitchen work surface (above) works beautifully together, for example. On the narrow ledge above the kitchen counter, a small group of treasured objects can become an individual still life within the larger scene (opposite). It all depends on how we choose to look at our home and the pieces that surround us.

FORAGING FROM NATURE

A dried flower, a tall summer grass, an abandoned bird's nest, a piece of wood – you name it, it's all there for us to notice and bring home to give our living space that extra layer of natural texture that I feel is so important. If a home lacks pieces collected in nature, it is missing the most important ingredient that any style of interior needs to make it a little more lived-in, less stark and slightly imperfect. The idea of 'perfection' doesn't appeal to me in the slightest – a home should be comfortable, relaxed and bear traces of life, with unique objects that can't be bought and natural pieces that you found on your travels and knew would sit well in a vase or on a sideboard as part of a still life.

NATURAL PORTRAITS.

My homes are full of treasures found on walks, on work trips or even in the garden. The beautiful bird's nest (opposite, left) was attached to a tall fallen fern in the forest in Sweden; it now lives in a large woven African bowl in Paris. I love the shape and colour of horns, which can be tied together with string to make an intriguing wall decoration (opposite, right). Every summer, when we arrive in the south of France, there are dried-out Christmas roses still standing and still lovely enough to display in a vase (below left). There are always some of the tall wild grasses that grow alongside paths and fields on a simple metal side table in our house (below right).

everyday vignettes

The next time you are going to take a photograph for Instagram, or just for yourself, zoom out a little and look at the bigger picture of a part of your home. You will soon see that you have many larger vignettes that, without you realizing it, have become everyday still lifes. It is easy to think of still lifes as just being collections of small items on a table or another surface, but they can also be on a larger scale and include pieces of furniture. Visiting the houses featured in this book, as well as some of the locations I have styled for photoshoots for work, I have often been amazed by how many large-scale vignettes people have in their homes.

COLLECTIONS ON DISPLAY.
I photographed a home in Portland, Oregon, for this book, and the whole interior consisted of such pleasing and carefully considered large-scale still lifes that I had to photograph them all (see pages 134–147). I love everything about this vignette (opposite and left) – the collections of old alarm clocks and vintage signs, the desk and the wooden and metal stool, all sitting so beautifully against the wood-panelled wall, which had been freshened up with a new coat of white paint but otherwise left in its original state.

BEAUTY ALL AROUND.
A place you use every day becomes a vignette when viewed through a camera. This desk area has unintentionally become a beautiful still life, almost as well composed as a painting (opposite). A pair of vintage leather and wooden chairs positioned in front of an old wooden storage unit topped with a collection of vintage items form an eye-catching arrangement (this page).

EVERYTHING GOES.
When creating a still life, you can choose a handful of related objects or random items that have nothing in common, you can stick to a colour palette or use similar materials. There is no right or wrong. Above is an example of unrelated items brought together to create a still life on a bedroom dresser/hutch. Opposite, on a simple wall shelf, a collection of small green glass bottles sits very well with vintage paintbrushes and books, creating a display that is uncomplicated but eye-catching.

At home with
Nature.

Natural
TEXTURES

Some places that you visit give you a particular feeling, while others convey a totally different vibe. When I entered this home in the middle of the medina in Marrakech, owned by Nicole, I instantly felt so calm and at ease that I could have moved in there and then.

   Not many places I visit make me feel that I never want to leave, but this home is everything I love down to the smallest detail. Every element has been so cleverly thought through and all the materials used have been sourced from nature. Could it get any better?

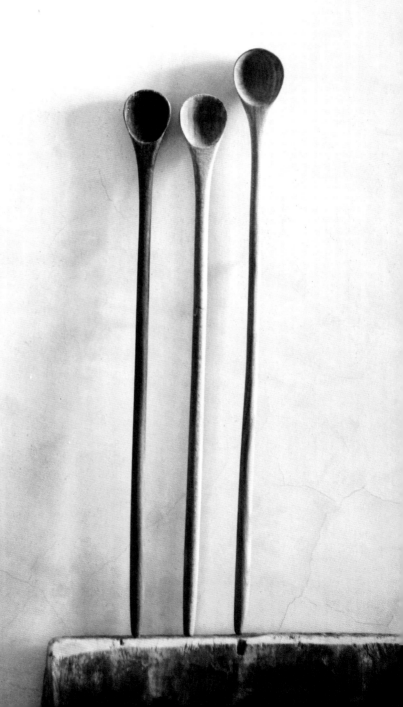

COMPLEMENTARY MATERIALS.
The main living area is on the second floor of the house. First, you enter the kitchen, situated between two wooden pillars, with an open-plan living and dining area beyond (opposite). The addition of lots of natural wood gives this otherwise sparsely decorated area a warm, inviting feeling. All the materials have been chosen to complement each other, including the smooth concrete floors and the Tadelakt plaster walls, a local technique that uses only natural materials.

When Nicole contacted me on Instagram and invited me to come and shoot her new home, which was just being finished, for my next book, I didn't hesitate for a second before replying with a very large and loud YES! From what I could gather from the photos she sent, mostly close-ups, I knew this house would be a perfect fit for the book as all the decorative elements and furnishings were natural and so well done and laid out. I had also seen pictures on Instagram of the riad that Nicole owns, which convinced me that her home was somewhere I needed to capture with my camera for the book. I don't know if I have ever felt such intense heat as we did while walking to meet Nicole for lunch before visiting her house, carrying heavy camera equipment and tripods through the narrow, crowded streets of the medina, but I am so happy that we visited the sweltering streets of Marrakech to photograph this beautiful house.

NATURAL ELEMENTS.
I love the Mauritanian Tuareg
mats, crafted from tightly
stitched palm straw and strips
of camel leather, that Nicole
has used throughout the house
to add texture to the concrete
floors (opposite, left). The sofas
in the living area are made
from mattresses covered in
neutral linen with matching
cushions (opposite, right).
A traditional cedarwood
Berber bread table and a
beautiful dried palm leaf make
a charming still life (this page).

IN ALL SIMPLICITY.

To keep your belongings to a bare minimum and live in a sparse, uncluttered space seems, to me, a brave and disciplined choice. I am too much of a collector to live in this way – I can't resist adding new pieces whenever I see something I love – but Nicole's home inspired me so much that I was tempted to go home and change everything! Although that didn't happen, I am considering making a simple yet comfortable sofa like Nicole's for my house in the south of France, as it would provide another bed for guests as well as an inviting place for a siesta.

OPEN-PLAN.
When Nicole took over the house it had many small rooms, which made it dark and hard to live in. With her talent for spatial planning, she knocked down the dividing walls to make each floor into one large, well-planned room. The kitchen became an open space, with the work surface and seating area dividing it from the main living area. I love the colours, textures and open storage solutions that Nicole created in her small but functional kitchen. The hanging rail for storing cooking pots, designed by Nicole and handcrafted by Rachid Bargamane, is a clever idea as it frees up both the work surface and cabinet space.

As soon as I walked off the winding streets of the medina and through the front door of this house, I felt it was going to be remarkable. And as I visited each floor (I don't think I closed my mouth once), I just knew the space would photograph beautifully and add another natural look that was totally different from the other homes featured in the book. Even though we are all good talkers, it didn't take me long to get my camera out and start shooting. Everywhere I looked was serene and full of beauty, with every single element of the natural look that I truly love. I am so grateful that Nicole reached out to me to photograph and feature her exquisite home in the heart of the bustling medina of Marrakech. I can't wait to return and spend more time developing our friendship. It is amazing where life takes you, and I feel so blessed at the stunning places I get to visit and the fascinating people I meet along the way.

CUSTOM-MADE.

The dining table was custom-made from a large, organic-shaped piece of aged wood found in a local flea market, with the metal support crafted to fit by Rachid Bargamane. The chairs were specially made by Cassandra Karinsky, and the raw wood bench will one day be raised to provide more seating. All the wooden pendant lamps in the house are from La Maison Pernoise in the south of France. The sculptural vase, by Soufiane Zarib, takes centre stage in this calm and serene space.

HARMONIOUS SLEEP.

On the first floor is Nicole's open-plan bedroom and bathroom area, which was originally two smaller rooms. The bathroom (see overleaf) occupies one section of the room and the rest of the space is devoted to the bedroom. The large windows ensure the room is filled with natural light, while the pure and simple design and furnishings create a tranquil space, where the soft grey walls, tonal bed linen and vintage wooden screens all work in harmony.

NATURALLY SEAMLESS.

Isn't this open-plan bathroom simply a dream? Its simplicity makes you want to stay and
pamper yourself all day. The design is so seamless, with all the elements melting into
each other. The walls, bathtub and sink are all made from Tadelakt plaster, a traditional
technique where lime plaster is rammed, polished and treated with soap to make it
waterproof and water-repellent – a perfect material for wet areas of the home (opposite).
The combination of the modern shower by Meir with the wooden elements makes this
bathroom feel both up-to-date and timeless (above left). I love the ingenious use of the
piece of dried bamboo that has been cut to form the water spout for the bathtub, which
is both beautiful and environmentally friendly (above right).

PRIVATE VIEW.

On the top floor is a roof terrace where Nicole can enjoy both the morning sun and the most beautiful sunsets over the rooftops of Marrakech. The space was designed by landscape architect Valentin Green, together with Nicole, and includes a small outdoor bathtub (below right), a seating area (below left) and a shower that you enter through an antique wooden door sourced locally (opposite). The terrace has the same seamless Tadelakt plaster finish as the rest of the house. For privacy, a simple metal structure was built on top of one wall to which Nicole added Mauritanian Tuareg mats, from Trésor Des Nomades, that fit the space naturally and add a different texture. There is the same attention to detail here as in the rest of this well-planned and inspirational home.

Harvest
OF BEAUTY

It is endlessly fascinating seeing
the kinds of things people choose
to collect. When I visited the home
of Lindsea and Danny in Portland,
Oregon, I knew I would see plenty of
interesting objects as they both buy
and sell antiques for their business,
House of Harvest. But the treasures
the couple have chosen to keep for
their own home tell a story of two
people with an amazing eye for
detail and a knack for uncovering
very special things that many people
wouldn't even notice.

CURATED WITH LOVE.
It takes a special skill to create a large still life like this one, made up
of vintage birdcages and old painting cases still filled with their paint
tubes and brushes (opposite). Lindsea and Danny retained the peeling
floral wallpaper on the walls as a reminder of the room's previous life.
The simple metal lamp (this page) has sculptural lines which mean
it works as a piece of art as well, bringing light to a dark corner.

We arrived in Portland, Oregon the day before we were going to photograph Lindsea and Danny's home, so I contacted Lindsea to ask for some tips on where to go and what to see. One thing led to another, and we arranged to meet up for dinner. We arrived at the restaurant a little early, filled with the mixture of nerves and excitement that comes when you are meeting people for the first time. But when Lindsea and Danny sat down and we started chatting, it felt as if we'd met many times before. One of the best things about my job is that it allows me to connect with so many interesting, like-minded people all over the world – something I appreciate greatly.

Early the next morning we drove through the countryside outside Portland towards Lindsea and Danny's house. As we approached, I could hardly contain my excitement as I realized we were about to walk into one of my dream houses – an old, typically American wooden farmhouse,

BEAUTIFULLY NEUTRAL.
The light and bright living room is the heart of the home. The cosy seating area is home to two sofas, a couple of antique chairs, an old white-painted wooden cabinet and a wood-burning stove that is lit every day throughout the winter to add atmosphere and keep the house warm (opposite). The room is decorated with personal objects and lots of natural elements such as branches, dried gourds and, of course, firewood ready for the stove (below left and right).

FLEA-MARKET FINDS.
The leather rocking armchair was found at a flea market along with the wooden cabinet that it lives beside (opposite). On top of the cabinet is a collection of vintage green glass bottles and oversized wooden chopping boards, creating a beautiful still life (this page).

painted white and set among trees and fields. I am a sucker for anything left untouched and untampered with, and one of the things that drew me to this location was that Lindsea and Danny have, as much as is possible, left their house in its original state, choosing to retain its character and just freshen it up here and there as needed.

Both inside and out, the couple have kept the original architectural details intact – the sash windows, mouldings and wood-panelled walls. The hardwood floors were restored and the walls given a wash of white paint. This beautiful interior is filled with Lindsea and Danny's treasures, thoughtfully collected over the years and now proudly displayed in their own home. Other pieces are in transit, ready to move on to new owners. It was hard to drag ourselves away from this warm and welcoming house, decorated with so much love and creativity.

FOOD WITH FRIENDS.
It took some time for Lindsea and Danny to find the right table for the dining room – one that was both large enough to cater for large gatherings and suited the space both in style and finish (opposite). The couple finally tracked down this piece – originally used as a prep table in a restaurant around the turn of the previous century, the surface has a beautiful patina of use. The white-painted vintage cabinet holds tableware and glasses and on top Lindsea has arranged an assortment of vintage treasures to create a textural still life (this page).

FARMHOUSE KITCHEN.

When entering the house you come in via a small but very light hallway (just glimpsed through the door) leading to the kitchen (opposite). Lindsea and Danny gave this space a gentle update, adding a concrete worksurface to the existing cabinetry and covering walls and cabinets with a coat of white paint. This is a true farmhouse kitchen, and every spare inch of space is adorned with hardworking vintage chopping boards, tableware, kitchenalia and linens. Not only is the kitchen beautifully arranged, it is also very practical, with frequently used items stored within reach of the stove top, sink and prep area (below, left and right). The natural textures of wood, china and metal add visual interest and make this a place you want to linger.

PILE IT HIGH.
At the other end of the kitchen is an old worktable with drawers that hold flatware and kitchen tools (opposite). The wooden shelf unit that stands on top was one of the very first things they bought for the farmhouse. Today it is home to plates, glasses, storage tins and an assortment of interesting kitchenalia, including vintage enamelware. The short wall at the end of the kitchen cabinets is home to a small wooden stool (this page). Storage baskets and kitchen towels hang from the wooden skirting above the tongue-and-groove wall.

SUNNY MORNINGS.

In the bedroom the walls are made of simple planking –
a favourite of mine as it brings life and texture to any room
(opposite and right). The bed is placed beneath the windows,
which are hung with unobtrusive plain white roller blinds. A
hand-turned wooden table stands beneath a homemade dream
catcher made from a birch branch with feathers and dried
herbs attached (above). On the other side of the corridor is the
bathroom, which underwent a few changes when the couple
moved in (above right). They added a flea-market sink on legs
and a wooden chest of drawers to store towels and toiletries.

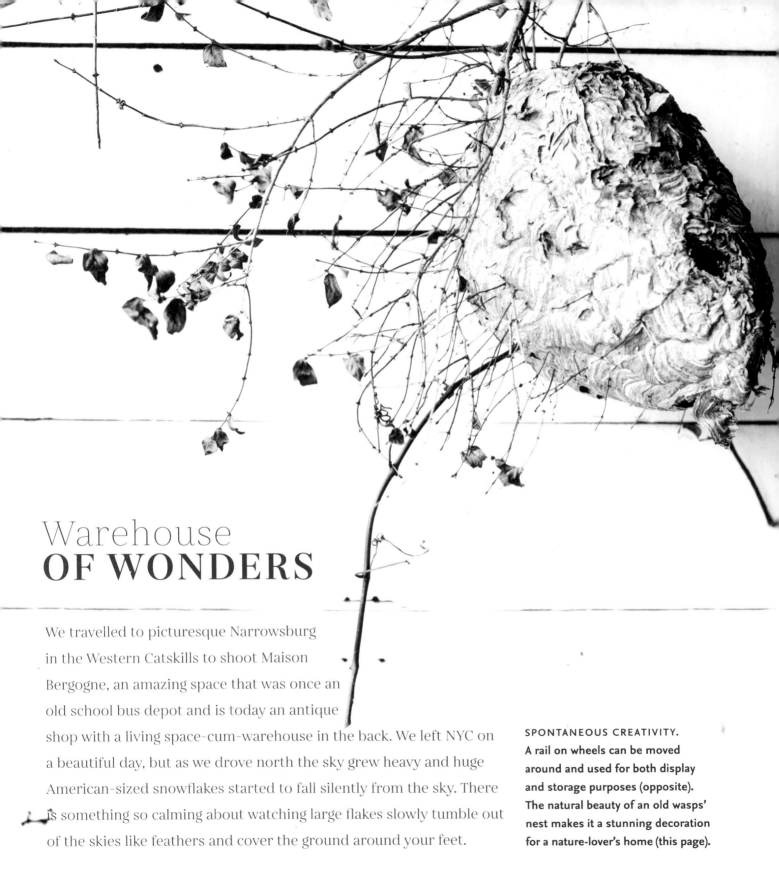

Warehouse
OF WONDERS

We travelled to picturesque Narrowsburg
in the Western Catskills to shoot Maison
Bergogne, an amazing space that was once an
old school bus depot and is today an antique
shop with a living space-cum-warehouse in the back. We left NYC on
a beautiful day, but as we drove north the sky grew heavy and huge
American-sized snowflakes started to fall silently from the sky. There
is something so calming about watching large flakes slowly tumble out
of the skies like feathers and cover the ground around your feet.

SPONTANEOUS CREATIVITY.
A rail on wheels can be moved
around and used for both display
and storage purposes (opposite).
The natural beauty of an old wasps'
nest makes it a stunning decoration
for a nature-lover's home (this page).

It was a magical feeling arriving at Maison Bergogne and walking towards the open garage door with snow falling thick and fast, covering the beautiful found objects and salvaged items that the owner, Juliette Hermant, had arranged around the entrance. Juliette was well wrapped up in multiple layers of clothing, gloves and heavy winter boots, and it was at this point that I realized I had not planned for the cold weather and that shooting in a place that was not heated was going to be a challenge, as I get cold very easily and really suffer from it. I knew that I would have to wear every single piece of clothing I had brought with me in order to be able to take photos that were sharp and focused, not blurry because I was shaking with cold while I was shooting!

However, when we entered the shop, it was packed with such an array of amazing and diverse antique and vintage objects that I was immediately distracted – an infinite variety of unique

SUSPENDED SEATING.
Isn't this suspended sofa an amazing idea (opposite and overleaf)? Layered with throws and suede pillows, it looks so inviting – the perfect spot for an afternoon nap. The seat is suspended with thick rope so that it can hold the weight of a few people. The open shelves in this area offer storage for plant pots, tools and other intriguing collectables (above left). At one end of the sofa, a salvaged shelving unit carries art materials such as paints and brushes (above right).

pieces were displayed and arranged with such creative flair. Marvelling at our surroundings, we walked through to the back of the shop, where Juliette has converted a warehouse into a liveable home. Even though it was so cold that I could see my own breath, I forgot the sub-zero temperatures in my excitement that I would be the one to shoot all this beauty! Wherever I looked, I felt an impulse to buy everything, then find a warehouse, loft space or barn and recreate this place for myself. I thought that such a dream-like place could only exist in my imagination.

Luckily the next morning the sturdy iron stove was roaring and Juliette had kindly brought tons of hot coffee to keep us warm. The day spent shooting here at Maison Bergogne was an unforgettable experience, allowing me to capture Juliette's many natural treasures and the unusual arrangements she has curated. Our visit was a true blessing.

PERFECTLY IMPERFECT.
I love everything about this kitchen – the antique industrial sink with the wooden table placed in front bring to mind a still life painting (opposite). The grey-painted cabinet to the right of the sink houses dry goods stored in glass jars along with other kitchenalia (below right), while the vintage ladder to the left of the sink holds kitchen towels. The beautiful lemon tart was made by Juliette (below left).

COVERED UP.

To the left of the small dining table, against a wood-panelled wall, stand shallow wooden shelving units holding everyday china and glassware ready for use. To cover the shelving unit and keep plates and glassware dust-free, Juliette has pinned up a vintage painting cloth, which adds another layer of visual interest and a different texture to the wood, porcelain and enamelled surface of the antique stove. Frequently used cooking utensils hang on vintage peg rails above the stove, within easy reach of anyone cooking.

SOMEWHERE TO SOAK.
Who wouldn't want to retreat here with a good book, a glass of wine, some lit candles and music playing in the background? I am not usually a bathtub kind of person, but this setting is so irresistible that I would probably climb into the tub and never want to get out again!

A COSY NEST.

An antique French metal bed is made up with down-filled blue-and-white French ticking pillows layered with a boldly coloured Native American handmade throw (opposite and above right). Such an inviting mix of things, created in very different places and with very different aesthetics, but they seem to have been designed for each other from the beginning. The small window over the bed has been fitted with slatted wooden shutters to keep the light out (opposite). The iron stove is in frequent use in winter, for its generous warmth, the crackling noise from the fire and the tang of woodsmoke (above left).

Eclectic
COLLECTORS

When I started work on this book, I knew I had
to include Ken and Mac's home. Not only is it
full of wonderful natural materials, colours and
textures, but it is so true to the personalities of
its owners. It's a home that's been made with love
and the contents reveal a deep-seated respect and
understanding of craftsmanship and beauty. For
me, one of its many charms is that not one single
piece of furniture or decorative object is new –
everything has been painstakingly tracked down
at flea markets and antiques fairs over the years.
This passion for old, rare and weathered pieces
is central to Ken and Mac's decorating philosophy,
but one huge additional benefit is that reusing and
recycling things that have already had one lifetime
is so much better for our planet.

LAYERED TEXTURES.
There are a few seating areas in the living room, each one different from the others, and
this one is my favourite (opposite). I love the elegant lines of the faux leather rocker covered
with an antique woven Navajo throw. The imposing wooden grandfather clock is French and
was found at an antiques market. The large Mexican jar behind the rocker was damaged in
one of the large earthquakes that occurred in this area in the 1980s but has been carefully
reconstructed and restored. A beautiful decorative piece made from found turkey feathers
and seed beads was created by Mac and inspired by Native American culture (this page).

LOOKING THROUGH THE LENS.
Mac and Ken's place was a joy to shoot.
An English Windsor chair is dressed
with a beautiful Navajo textile (left).
The small sabino wood table was found
in Mexico, while the pencil box is by
artist Larry Blagg (above). This antique
marquetry desk was found at the Rose
Bowl Flea Market in Pasadena, a place
where Ken and Mac often go to look
for antiques (opposite).

When I visited Ken and Mac in Los Feliz, Los Angeles, for the first time, I wasn't quite sure what to
expect of them or their home. I had 'met' Ken via Instagram only a few months earlier. At the time,
I was about to visit Los Angeles for the first time for a job, and I was feeling super-excited and
curious about the trip. When going to a new place for work, it's always hard to know where to source
the right props for the job. But by a great stroke of luck Ken started to follow me on Instagram, then
I reciprocated and soon realized that we shared an interest in antiques and flea-market finds as well
as all sorts of unusual, whimsical and salvaged pieces. Without any hesitation, I messaged Ken to ask
if he could kindly give me some tips on the best places to track down eclectic items and interesting
objects, and every single recommendation he made turned out to be exactly what I was looking for.
A social media story with a happy ending!

CABINET OF CURIOSITIES.
The elegant Louis Seize loveseat just seen on the right-hand side (above) was inherited from a friend, while the French-style chair and small flip table were found at a flea market. The table was only $35 – as Mac says, early birds get the prize! The antique Mexican table was purchased on one of the couple's trips to Santa Fe and on top sits an array of favourite finds amassed over the years (opposite).

We stayed in contact and when we arrived in LA, Ken invited us over to the couple's house for a drink and then dinner at one of their favourite restaurants. Without hesitation I said yes. I had a feeling we would get along and I'm also far too curious to turn down an offer to visit someone's home!

Our first visit to Ken and Mac's house was a case of love at first sight. Not only did we immediately click with the couple themselves, but when I walked into their home I was totally smitten. The interior is a collector's paradise, a world of beautiful things displayed with a discerning eye. The décor is simple, allowing the antiques and other pieces to take centre stage. Every corner holds something that intrigues the eye and begs you to look closer. I could spend weeks here, hearing the stories behind each and every object. Yet, despite the many rare and unique pieces, this still feels like a cosy and comfortable home. I drew so much inspiration from Ken and Mac's home, and I hope you will, too.

TAKE A SEAT.
A corner of the living room is home to a French-style wing chair upholstered in faux lizard skin and layered with antique Japanese fabric. The wooden footstool was found at a flea market and the tin wall sconces were brought back from Mexico (opposite). The blue window shutters originally came from the historic Bullock's Wilshire store in Los Angeles (below left). On top of the fireplace is a pair of jars from Tonala in Mexico. The view from the front door is of this French armoire, which fits perfectly between two windows (below right).

INTRIGUING DISPLAYS.

In the dining room, a large round table is the centrepiece (opposite). The base is made from the trunk of an old cypress tree, while the table top is black African granite with bull-nose edges. I was lucky to capture a glimpse of Bella the dog, a mix of Italian greyhound and whippet. Ken and Mack found this wooden table, originally from the Happy Bottom Riding Club in the Mojave desert, 35 years ago at an antiques shop in Pasadena (below left). The antique Santo statue with the straw hat was bought from Lawry's California Center in their closing-down sale. The pie buffet is English and dates from the nineteenth century, home to a large iron urn filled with various seashells found at flea markets (below right). The painting above is by James M. Hart, a landscape painter and member of the Hudson River School.

A PLACE TO DREAM. The main bedroom is on the second floor and is entered via a narrow flight of steps. The bed is dressed in loose linens and layered with antique Navajo textiles. Above hangs a painting by Californian artist Frank L. Sandford.

HANG YOUR HAT.
The open shelving unit in the
bedroom holds a collection
of baskets, pottery and several
Mexican retablos. Above,
a collection of cowboy hats
hangs from a vintage Mexican
steer-horn hat rack.

VARIED TREASURES.

In the bedroom, one of the bedside tables/nightstands is a vintage Monterey Furniture Prohibition era 'hidden bar' – the cowhide-covered top lifts off to reveal a secret compartment in the back where it was possible to hide liquor bottles (above left). The teal-coloured wooden chest was once used to hold oats for horses but today provides extra storage (above right). On the wall above is a Northwest Coast Native American mask and antique Native American baskets. The iron wall sconce is original to the house, which was built in 1933. The hickory wood chair with a caned seat originally came from the Del Mar racetrack and was found by Mac in an antiques store. A few steps up from the bedroom is the tower room, which houses a treasured collection of Ozark roadside tourist pottery (opposite). There are more than 75 pieces collected over 40 years. The sun-faded metal folding chair was found at a flea market and originally came from a 1940s motel.

Beautifully
SIMPLE

In a hilltop village in the southwest of
France, tucked away on a narrow lane,
stands Camellas-Lloret, a very special
B&B and the home of Annie Moore and
her husband Colin. I was eager to visit
their amazing home, hidden behind
a high wall in the centre of the village,
and capture it for this book. I am lucky
enough to visit many beautiful homes
when photographing for my books
and in my work as an art director and
stylist, and it's hard to describe the
feeling of excitement as I stand waiting
for the homeowner to open the door
and invite me in, allowing me to see
their world through my own eyes.

PERFECTLY STACKED.
Entering the home of Annie and Colin, you are greeted by the most
perfectly stacked wall of firewood (opposite). This is Colin's creation,
and Annie told us how proud he is of his handiwork. The entrance
hall has large windows that provide a glimpse of the walled garden.

Walking into an unknown interior and meeting the owners for the first time is nerve-racking and exhilarating at the same time. I imagine all sorts of scenarios: will we get along, will the owners let me photograph what I want, will we be able to make a cup of coffee… All these fleeting thoughts run through my head, yet seconds later a new connection has been made and you know that everything is going to flow perfectly. Meeting Annie for the first time was just like that – easy and fun. I guess there is something in the stars that brings you to certain places and to certain people. We even discovered that before Annie and Colin moved to Camellas-Lloret they owned a house very close to our own in the south of France, yet despite knowing many of the same people we had never met. In fact, we had so much to chat about that I thought I wouldn't get any photography done if I didn't stop talking!

SITTING SOFTLY.
The sitting room is a warm, welcoming space (opposite). The rusty pink sofa is from Bed & Philosophy and its boxy shape echoes that of the wooden coffee table. On a rough-hewn block of wood stands an oversized glass lamp topped with a lampshade made from faux suede (above left). The painted table is a flea-market find, home to a pile of books and a flower or branch from the garden (above right).

Annie and Colin's style is perfectly in tune with my own. Their house shows their passion for natural materials and contrasting textures, and every corner has its own personal touch. The large, high-ceilinged rooms, with their beautiful original architectural detailing, are full of objects and treasures that the couple have amassed over the years, many of them found at flea markets and car boot/yard sales or discovered in skips/dumpsters and then carried with the couple from place to place until they find the perfect home. Antique and vintage pieces sit happily next to modern and retro designs, and the colour palette includes my favourite rich, earthy hues. Annie and Colin's creative talents mean that Camellas-Lloret is every bit as warm, easy and comfortable as the company of its owners.

NATURAL TEXTURES.
In the dining room the walls are painted with lime paint from Bauwerk Colour. Its velvety texture provides a beautiful, natural backdrop to the objects on the sideboards placed each side of the dining table. Vintage cake stands are mixed with wooden chopping boards and white ceramic bowls, and an antique ceramic urn holds large branches of eucalyptus. The square wall lamp was made by Colin from MDF and painted in the same colour as the wall (opposite).

A PLACE TO GATHER.
I think round or oval dining tables are the best shape for sociable dinner parties. This marble-topped oval table takes centre stage in the dining room, and the number of chairs and stools varies according to how many people are sitting down to eat (opposite). The part-glazed cabinet that occupies nearly a whole wall was custom-made for the space by Colin, using old doors and windows found when a neighbour's house was cleared out (above). It's so in tune with the rest of the room that it looks as if it's been here forever.

SHADES OF GREY.
One of the four guestrooms is painted a very soft grey colour. The bed is positioned below the large windows and the rest of the room is very sparsely furnished with a low side table and a modern lamp providing some contrast to the natural textures in the room (this page). A peg rail painted in the same colour as the wall provides extra storage for clothes as well as decorative items (opposite).

TONES AND TEXTURES.

The main bedroom is simply decorated with a calm and soothing vibe. The colour scheme here is neutral with subtle touches of soft pink. Visual interest also comes from the contrasting natural textures – the bed is made from rough-hewn wood with logs for legs, the bed linen is washed linen and a shaggy rug covers the tiled floor. Even in this simple, tranquil space, Annie and Colin's personalities shine through. The wood used to make the bed was found in and around the house, as the previous owner enjoyed woodwork and left many of his raw materials behind when he left. The lamps on the walls are the same as in the dining room, made by Colin from MDF, then painted the same colour as the walls.

BE MY GUEST.
Another tranquil guest bedroom (this page). An antique French metal bed inbetween two windows is the perfect place to read a book or just relax while listening to the birds singing in the trees outside the window. The mirror above the marble fireplace is made out of many small mirrored squares (opposite). I love the way the man in the antique oil painting seems to be gazing out at the room.

Rustic
RETREAT

At the end of the garden at the Camellas-Lloret B&B near
Carcassonne, France, stands a small house that owners Annie
and Colin Moore call 'the apartment'. I would describe it as
a small townhouse, since the cosy space is spread over three
storeys. Even though the floorspace is limited, it is still a
house in its own right, and would make a perfect weekend
retreat. I particularly wanted to include the apartment in
the book because it boasts so many creative ideas that are
relevant for anyone living in a smaller home.

TREASURES OF NATURE.
I am slightly obsessed with birds'
nests and this one in Annie's house
is particularly beautiful (this page). On
a shallow windowsill is a collection of
small succulents – the perfect plant for
a weekend house, as they don't mind
a little neglect and will live for quite
some time without water (opposite).

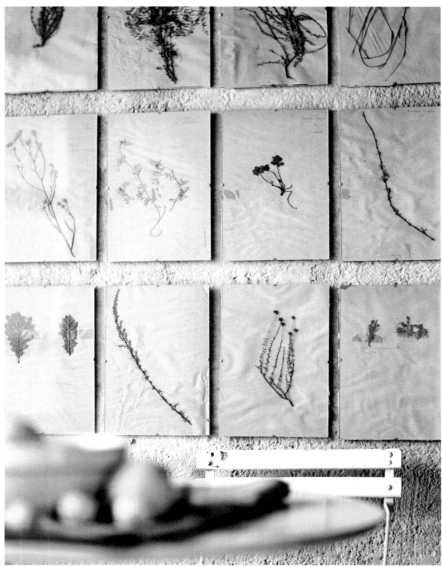

MIX AND MATCH.
From the garden, you enter the apartment through glazed doors that lead into the dining and kitchen area. The dining table and matching stools were found at a flea market, and simple folding garden chairs were added to create more seating. The wall display was created by framing vintage pressed flowers in simple glass clip frames and hanging them in a grid formation.

Annie and Colin made the decision not to carry out too much redecoration or refurbishment in this little house, instead aiming to retain its simple rustic charm. The roughly plastered walls have been gently updated with a coat of paint in places, while original aged terracotta tiles cover the floors. Tactile textiles add a note of luxury. As a result, the interior has a serene, timeless feel and a restful atmosphere – just what you need at a weekend retreat.

The apartment has been furnished with many found objects as well as pieces sourced at local flea markets and items made by the owners, yet it has the feeling that everything in it was bought to fit the space perfectly. Of course, you can't always find exactly what you're looking for when you go vintage or antique-hunting – that's part of the fun – but with a bit of imagination you can generally find something similar or with the same function. I believe that it's possible to furnish a house without buying anything brand new, instead seeking out items that have already had a previous life, used and owned by someone else prior to you. We humans produce so much waste and cause so much damage to the planet that I believe recycling and reusing is the way forward, rather than buying new things as soon as we fancy a change. There are flea markets, antiques markets and car boot/yard sales all over the world where you can find just the thing you need to update your home. Don't forget online auction sites like eBay, where many find unique pieces. There are even 'freecycling' organizations that make it easy to give away unwanted but reusable items to those who need them.

The only thing I would always buy new is a bed – they are a very personal choice and different beds suit different bodies. Not to mention that the average mattress has a lifespan of only about ten years. When it comes to everything else, there is no reason not to reuse and recycle.

HOME MADE.
The two sofas positioned at right angles in the sitting room were made by Annie using mattresses found at a local flea market and reupholstered in vintage white linen (opposite). The cushion covers were crafted from old linen sheets and artists' canvas (below). Simple divan/box spring sofas like these are a practical idea if you live in a smaller space, and can double up as guest beds when needed. The pendant lamp was decorated with tassels and painted with gesso to match the whitewashed walls.

OPEN STORAGE.
In a small space, wall shelves offer lots of valuable storage space for books, magazines, collectables and other decorative pieces. These shelves were made using simple brackets and planks of wood painted white so that they melt into the wall and let the items on display take centre stage.

LIKE A DREAM.

Isn't this bedroom a dream? The soft light filtering through the window and the canopy above the bed create
a tranquil, magical atmosphere. The bed canopy was made from muslin/cheesecloth bought in Atlanta more
than 30 years ago, and an old hula hoop was used to create the framework. Most people would have thrown
away the fabric many years ago, but Annie knew that one day it would come in useful. Colin made the bed
to fit the space, using reclaimed wood found at the property or salvaged from skips/dumpsters.

A PLACE TO HIDE.
Attached to the apartment is a greenhouse-like space overlooking the garden (opposite). It's a chilled hideaway where you can hang out on cooler days or when it's raining outside while still enjoying the garden views. Colin and Annie have furnished the room very simply, with an antique sofa and a coffee table made from salvaged planks of wood resting on old trestles. White-painted shelves are home to a collection of large green bottles and an array of succulent plants (above). Simple, timeless perfection.

picture credits

All photography by Hans Blomquist

2 The Swedish home of interior stylist and decorator Marie Olsson Nylander www.mointerior.com; 3 Annie Moore www.camellaslloret.com; 5 Atelier KECHYOTO – a private home in the Souks of the Marrakech Medina, owned and designed by Nicole Francesca Manfron/Nicole Francesca Manfron DESIGN – The Secret Souk; 6 left The home of antique dealers Lindsea & Danny Dragomir of HouseofHarvest.com; 6 right Atelier KECHYOTO – a private home in the Souks of the Marrakech Medina, owned and designed by Nicole Francesca Manfron/ Nicole Francesca Manfron DESIGN – The Secret Souk; 7 left The seasonal quarters and shop of Juliette Hermant of maisonbergogne.com; 7 right The home of antique dealers Lindsea and Danny Dragomir of HouseofHarvest.com; 20 Debi Treloar www.debitreloar.com; 22 right Debi Treloar www.debitreloar.com; 29 The seasonal quarters and shop of Juliette Hermant of maisonbergogne.com; 30 The home of antique dealers Lindsea and Danny Dragomir of HouseofHarvest.com; 33 Bauwerk Colour www.bauwerk.co.au; 34 Annie Moore www.camellaslloret.com; 37 right Annie Moore www.camellaslloret.com; 44–45 Atelier KECHYOTO – a private home in the Souks of the Marrakech Medina, owned and designed by Nicole Francesca Manfron/ Nicole Francesca Manfron DESIGN – The Secret Souk; 49 Bauwerk Colour www.bauwerk.co.au; 51 Bauwerk Colour www.bauwerk.co.au; 54 left The Swedish home of interior stylist and decorator Marie Olsson Nylander www.mointerior.com; 55 The Swedish home of interior stylist and decorator Marie Olsson Nylander www.mointerior.com; 56–57 Bauwerk Colour www.bauwerk.co.au; 58 left Bauwerk Colour www.bauwerk.co.au; 60–61 Bauwerk Colour www.bauwerk.co.au; 62 The Swedish home of interior stylist and decorator Marie Olsson Nylander www.mointerior.com; 64 left Annie Moore www.camellaslloret.com; 64 right Bauwerk Colour www.bauwerk.co.au; 65 left Annie Moore www.camellaslloret.com; 68 The home of antique dealers Lindsea and Danny Dragomir of HouseofHarvest.com; 70 The seasonal quarters and shop of Juliette Hermant of maisonbergogne.com; 71 above Atelier KECHYOTO – a private home in the Souks of the Marrakech Medina, owned and designed by Nicole Francesca Manfron/Nicole Francesca Manfron DESIGN – The Secret Souk; 73 right Atelier KECHYOTO designed by

Nicole Fancesca Manfron/Nicole Francesca Manfron DESIGN – The Secret Souk; 75 right Atelier KECHYOTO – a private home in the Souks of the Marrakech Medina, owned and designed by Nicole Francesca Manfron/ Nicole Francesca Manfron DESIGN – The Secret Souk; 77 right Atelier KECHYOTO – a private home in the Souks of the Marrakech Medina, owned and designed by Nicole Francesca Manfron/ Nicole Francesca Manfron DESIGN – The Secret Souk; 78 left Bauwerk Colour www.bauwerk.co.au; 79 Bauwerk Colour www.bauwerk.co.au; 80 right Atelier KECHYOTO – a private home in the Souks of the Marrakech Medina, owned and designed by Nicole Francesca Manfron/ Nicole Francesca Manfron DESIGN – The Secret Souk; 83 Annie Moore www.camellaslloret.com; 88–89 left Annie Moore www.camellaslloret.com; 91 Annie Moore www.camellaslloret.com; 98 left The home of Ken and Mac in Los Feliz; 98 right Annie Moore www.camellaslloret.com; 99–100 The seasonal quarters and shop of Juliette Hermant of maisonbergogne.com; 101 Atelier KECHYOTO – a private home in the Souks of the Marrakech Medina, owned and designed by Nicole Francesca Manfron/ Nicole Francesca Manfron DESIGN – The Secret Souk; 105 right The home of Ken and Mac in Los Feliz; 106–107 The seasonal quarters and shop of Juliette Hermant of maisonbergogne.com; 110–111 The home of antique dealers Lindsea and Danny Dragomir of HouseofHarvest.com; 112 The seasonal quarters and shop of Juliette Hermant of maisonbergogne.com; 113–115 The home of antique dealers Lindsea and Danny Dragomir of HouseofHarvest.com; 116–133 Atelier KECHYOTO – a private home in the Souks of the Marrakech Medina, owned and designed by Nicole Francesca Manfron/ Nicole Francesca Manfron DESIGN – The Secret Souk; 134–147 The home of antique dealers Lindsea and Danny Dragomir of Houseof Harvest. com; 148–159 The seasonal quarters and shop of Juliette Hermant of maisonbergogne.com; 160–161 Le Petite Cabine of Anie Stanley/Smokey Belles Catskills; 162–175 The home of Ken and Mac in Los Feliz; 176–201 Annie Moore www.camellaslloret. com; 203 above Atelier KECHYOTO – a private home in the Souks of the Marrakech Medina, owned and designed by Nicole Francesca Manfron/ Nicole Francesca Manfron DESIGN – The Secret Souk.; 203 below The seasonal quarters and shop of Juliette Hermant of maisonbergogne.com.

business credits

Annie Moore
Camellas-Lloret
E: anniemooredesign@
gmail.com
T: +33 (0)645739642
www.camellaslloret.com
IG: @camellaslloret
*Pages 3, 34, 37 right, 64 left,
65 left, 83, 88–89, 91, 176–201.*

Bauwerk Colour
Haupstrasse 15
04874 Belgern-Schildau
Germany
E: info@bauwerkcolour.co.uk
www.bauwerkcolour.co.uk
IG: @bauwerkcolour
*Pages 33, 49, 51, 56, 57, 58 left,
60–61, 64 right, 78 left, 79.*

Debi Treloar
www.debitreloar.com
Pages 20, 22 right.

House of Harvest
Antique farmhouse decor
for the well-collected home.
www.houseofharvest.com
IG: @houseofharvest
*Pages 6 left, 7 right, 30, 68,
110–111, 113–115, 134–147.*

Maison Bergogne
226 Bridge Street
Narrowsburg, NY 12764
USA
T: +1 (213) 379 3900
E: jh@maisonbergogne.com
www.maisonbergogne.com
IG: @maisonbergogne
With special thanks to
Vandelinde Antiques

Narrowsburg, NY 12764
T: +1 (570) 729-8402
and for the antique rugs
and coverlets,
Donna Endres collection
at The Campton Gallery
422 East Front Street,
Hancock, NY 13783
E: jlb@thecamptons.com
www.thecamptons.com
*Pages 7 left, 29, 70, 99, 100,
106–107, 112, 148–161, 203.*

Marie Olsson Nylander
Interior stylist, decorator,
antique lover
E: marie@mointerior.com
www.mointerior.com
IG: @marieolssonnylander
Pages 2, 54 left, 55, 62.

Nicole Francesca Manfron
DESIGN
E: Francesca.manfron@
hotmail.com

La Maison Marrakech
www.airbnb.com/
rooms/411375
IG: @la_maison_marrakech
IG: @thesecretsouk
IG: @nicxxxdesign
*Pages 5, 6 right, 44–45, 71
above, 73 right, 75 right, 77
right, 80 right, 116–133, 203.*

Smokey Belles Catskills
1914 County Road 23
Narrowsburg, NY 12764
USA
IG: Smokeybellescatskills
Pages 160, 161.

address book

UNITED STATES

LOS ANGELES

Big Daddy's Antiques
3334 La Cienega Place
Los Angeles, CA 90016
*Big Daddy's Antiques offers
a one-of-a-kind antiques and
reproductions from Europe,
Asia and North America. It is
truly inspiring to visit and
explore this store as it is
always changing and the
décor is just beautiful.*

The Good Liver
705 Mateo Street
Los Angeles, CA 90021
www.good-liver.com
*The Good Liver is a modern
version of a general store,
offering timeless and good
quality items sourced from
around the world. You can
find everything from garden
implements to toothpaste.*

Mart Collective
1600 Lincoln Blvd
Venice, CA 90291
www.themartcollective.com
*My favourite antiques and
vintage market. I always find
the best props here when I am
shooting in Los Angeles.*

Rolling Greens
9528 Jefferson Blvd
Culver City, CA 90232
www.rghomeandgarden.com
*A fantastic garden centre
where I source plants to use
on photo shoots. They also
have a downtown location
which also has a great retail
showroom full of beautiful
homewares and furniture.*

Tortoise General Store
12701 Venice Blvd,
Los Angeles, CA 90066
www.tortoiselife.com
*Advocates of a slow and steady
life, the Tortoise General Store
offers a curated selection of
timeless Japanese home goods
with a story behind each one.
It also doubles as a gallery
space for a wide range of
events and workshops.*

TUCSON, ARIZONA

Bon Boutique
760 S Stone Ave,
Tucson, AZ 85701
www.bon-boutique.com
*Owners Bonnie and Crystal
offers a collection of objects
that are well made and well
designed, sourced from
different corners of the world.
Their range offers both newly
made pieces as well as vintage
and antique items.*

NEW YORK

ABC Carpet and Home
888 Broadway,
New York, NY 10003
www.abchome.com
*This store is a must-visit
when I visit NYC. It is always
so inspiring, full of tempting
furniture and objects from
all over the world.*

BDDW
5 Crosby Street
New York, NY 10013
www.bddw.com
*BDDW is a small American
furniture company dedicated
to the creation of well-crafted
timeless designs by the
company's founder Tyler Hays.
Each piece is made in Tyler's
studio in Philadelphia.*

M. Crow
16 Howard St
New York, NY 10013
www.mcrowcompany.com
*Mostly clothing, but also
furniture and objects. A
favourite store of mine – I love
the philopsophy behind it as
the owner Tyler Hays says
'M. Crow is an awkward
collision of all my hobbies
and interest...I am basically
making from scratch the things
I want or need and making
extras and trying to sell them'.*

Goods for the Study
234 Mulberry Street
New York, NY 10012
www.mcnallyjacksonstore.com
*The best selection of stationery,
from notebooks to writing
tools to cards, desk accessories
to carriers and cases. It's hard
not to want everything! Also
some elegant pieces of office
furniture and desk lighting.*

Green Fingers Market
5 Rivington Street
New York, NY 10002
*A mix of plants and vintage
homeware, and a great
selection of vintage clothing.*

Roman and Williams Guild
53 Howard Street
New York, NY 10013
www.rwguild.com
*A collection of original lighting,
accessories and furniture
created by the Roman and
Williams design studio as well
as pieces from the workshops
of the world's best artisans.
There's also a French café,
La Mercerie. The best of
everything!*

Paula Rubenstein
21 Bond Street
New York, NY 10012
www.paularubenstein.com
*Paula's eponymous store is
a treasure trove of decorative
and functional vintage and
antique items for the home.
Set aside plenty of time to
browse here.*

FRANCE

MARSEILLE
Maison Empereur
4 Rue des Récolettes
13001 Marseille
*A hardware store that was
founded in 1827 and still most
likely looks exactly as it did
then. Here you will find anything
from tools to brushes to lamps
to textiles to ceramics to kids
toys and games. A treasure
chest to roam around.*

PERNES-LES-FONTAINES
La Maison Pernoise
167 Avenue de la Gare
84210 Pernes-les-Fountains
*This shop sells most things for
the home: furniture, lamps,
glassware, dinnerware and
baskets. All curated and chosen
to fit this shop. Perfect for
anyone who wants to create
a natural interior.*

PARIS
Astier de Villatte
173 Rue Saint-Honore
75001 Paris
*Beautifully crafted ceramics
with a very creative twist.*

L'Object qui Parle
86 Rue de Martyrs
75018 Paris
*My favourite vintage/antique
shop in Paris. Here you can
find some very interesting
objects – it is a bit like walking
into a cabinet de curiosité.*

SWEDEN

STOCKHOLM
Dusty Deco
Brahegatan 21
11437 Stockholm
www.dustydeco.com
*Edin, the shop owner, travels
the world to find extraordinary
treasures and bring them back
to his beautiful shop. It's a
great mix of furniture, objects
and art.*

Dry Studios
Upplandsgatan 36
11328 Stockholm
www.drystudios.com
*Their beautiful prints
of natural objects would look
good in any home.*

UNITED KINGDOM

HASTINGS
A G Hendy & Co
36 High Street
Hastings TN34 3ER
www.aghendy.com
*A beautiful shop in an old
Georgian townhouse, where
you just want to move in.
A large range of homewares
including vintage tableware,
candles, tools, buckets, antique
glassware and linens.*

ROSS-ON-WYE
Baileys Home
Whitecross Farm
Bridstow
Ross-on-Wye HR9 6JU
www.baileyshome.com
*At this rustic store housed in a
series of old farm buildings,
you will find a collection of
well-designed, well-made,
useful and uncomplicated
pieces for the home.*

RYE
Alex MacArthur Interiors
The Monastery
Conduit Hill
Rye TN31 7LE
www.alexmacarthur.co.uk
*The Monastery contains an
amazing collection of antiques
all beautifully set up in this
incredible building. Open by
appointment only.*

OXFORD
Objects of Use
6 Lincoln House
Market Street
Oxford OX1 3EQ
www.objectsofuse.com
*A modern-day hardware store
stocked with beautifully made,
practical items sourced from
around the globe.*

PAINT

Bauwerk colour
www.bauwerkcolour.com
*My favourite paint company.
I love their lime paint and the
range of colours is just
exquisite. It seems like they
have captured every hue of the
natural world. Their paint is
also eco-friendly, made from
clay, minerals and beautiful
natural pigments.*

index

Page numbers in *italic* refer to the illustrations

thank you

FREDERICK.
Without your help, this book would never have been done. It is amazing how you can bring out the very best in me, yet still do everything you do both in our home and when we work together nearly every day of the year. You are simply the best in every possible way. Your attention to detail amazes me and makes me work even harder, getting even better pictures. How lucky am I to get to spend everyday with you and travel the world experiencing new places and meeting new people? Exploring the world together is a gift. You are the sunshine.

MY PARENTS.
You are simply the most amazing! Thank you for everything you do for me, Frederick and Felix everyday, and for all the love and support. *Jag älskar er.*

BRONWYN AND ANDREAS AT BAUWERK COLOUR.
Thank you for being such dear friends and amazing people, and for letting me come and use your home as a photographic studio. I love spending time with you and being a small part of your amazing paint collection.

MIKKEL VANG.
Thank you for always lending me your junior tripod when I am too lazy to bring one along, and for being a superstar friend!

ANNABEL MORGAN.
You are a superstar editor! Thank you for always making my books better and better, and for all the positive and happy energy and support you give me while working on them.

CINDY, LESLIE, MEGAN, ZIA AND JESS.
We did it! Thank you for all the support and for pushing me to get on and finish the book. Without you, I would still be working on it!

THE HOMEOWNERS.
Thank you for so generously opening the doors to your homes, for letting us being there and for offering coffee and lunch and dinners, as well as sharing stories and allowing us to be part of your worlds for a few days. I am truly grateful, and I hope you will all be happy with the way your homes turned out in the book.